T0268627

SAVE the CLIMATE

THIS EDITION
Editorial Management by Oriel Square
Produced for DK by WonderLab Group LLC
Jennifer Emmett, Erica Green, Kate Hale, *Founders*

Editors Grace Hill Smith, Libby Romero, Maya Myers, Michaela Weglinski;
Photography Editors Kelley Miller, Annette Kiesow, Nicole di Mella; **Managing Editor** Rachel Houghton;
Designers Project Design Company; **Researcher** Michelle Harris; **Copy Editor** Lori Merritt;
Indexer Connie Binder; **Proofreader** Larry Shea; **Reading Specialist** Dr. Jennifer Albro;
Curriculum Specialist Elaine Larson

Published in the United States by DK Publishing
1745 Broadway, 20th Floor, New York, NY 10019

Copyright © 2023 Dorling Kindersley Limited
DK, a Division of Penguin Random House LLC
23 24 25 26 10 9 8 7 6 5 4 3 2 1
001-334012-July/2023

A catalog record for this book
is available from the Library of Congress.
HC ISBN: 9780-7440-7352-2
PB ISBN: 9780-7440-7353-9

DK books are available at special discounts when purchased in bulk for sales promotions, premiums,
fundraising, or educational use. For details, contact: DK Publishing Special Markets,
1745 Broadway, 20th Floor, New York, NY 10019
SpecialSales@dk.com

Printed and bound in China

The publisher would like to thank the following for their kind permission to reproduce their images:
a=above; c=center; b=below; l=left; r=right; t=top; b/g=background

123RF.com: Witold Kaszkin 19cra, nerthuz 3cb, yasonya 23t; **Alamy Stock Photo:** Robertharding / Tony Waltham 10; **Dreamstime.
com:** Valentin M Armianu 9, Darren Baker 29, Ali Ender Birer 1cb, Galuniki 28br, Štěpán Kápl 20crb, Karynf4 22, Andrey Koturanov
12bl, Glenn Rogers 17tl, Rosshelen 26b, Toa555 16b, Vlabos 11br; **Getty Images:** Digital Vision / Lauren Nicole 17br, Jim Dyson 25t,
LightRocket / SOPA Images 24t, Stone / TED MEAD 13br; **Getty Images / iStock:** amriphoto 8bl, appledesign 4-5, Neurobite 18-19t;
Shutterstock.com: AleksandarMilutinovic 7crb, ArchonCodex 13tl, aydngvn 6-7, Olga Miltsova 27tr, Wildeside 12br, Ziablik 14-15l;
Cover images: *Front:* **Shutterstock.com:** FloridaStock

All other images © Dorling Kindersley
For more information see: www.dkimages.com

For the curious
www.dk.com

SAVE the CLIMATE

Jen Szymanski

Contents

How Is Our Planet Changing?

A day at the beach is always a treat. But what if you arrived and saw this? The clear blue water you were expecting is foamy and brown. You can see gloopy patches of slime floating on top of the waves. The ocean is covered with sea snot! Yuck! Why is this happening?

The ocean is getting warmer, and it is changing. And it's not just the oceans. Temperatures all around Earth are on the rise. This is causing all sorts of changes to take place. Glaciers are melting. Sea levels are rising. Droughts and floods are becoming more common. Scientists believe all of this is happening because of climate change.

Slimy Waters
Sea snot isn't the same stuff that comes out of your nose when you have a cold. This slime is made by algae when ocean water gets warmer.

Climate is the pattern of weather in an area over a period of years. It includes things like how much snow and rain a place gets and how high and low the temperatures are there.

Climate change is a change in the usual weather patterns for a place. It can also be an overall change in Earth's climate. One example of climate change is a change in the average temperature for a place during a certain time of year. Another example is a change in the amount of rain or snow an area typically receives.

Weather or Climate?
The difference between weather and climate is time. Weather is what atmospheric conditions are like over a short period of time. Climate is how the atmosphere behaves over a long period of time.

The Sahara has one of the driest climates on Earth.

Briksdal Glacier, Norway
2002

Briksdal Glacier, Norway
2011

Earth's climate has always changed over time. That's nothing new. But the way Earth's climate is changing now is different, and scientists think people are to blame.

Scientists have lots of evidence that Earth's climate isn't the same as it was in the past. One obvious sign of that is global warming. Temperatures in most places on Earth have gone up about 1.8° F (1° C) in the past few centuries. That might not sound like a lot, but it's enough to cause a lot of changes.

A slight increase in Earth's average temperature causes ice and snow to melt. It causes glaciers to shrink. Glaciers all over the world have been melting more quickly. Some have disappeared completely.

All of that water from melting glaciers has to go somewhere. It runs down the slopes of hills and mountains and flows into the sea. It's a big reason the sea level rises every year. Scientists think the sea will rise along the United States coast at least 12 inches (0.3 m) by 2050.

As the sea level rises, the landscape changes. Land washes away. Coastlines move inland as oceans expand. Homes and buildings on the coast flood. They can be lost to the sea.

drought

flood

Changes in Ecosystems
Water running downhill picks up soil and carries it into streams and rivers. The dirt makes the water cloudy. This makes it harder for fish to breathe in the water.

While there is too much water in some places, there is too little in others. Long periods with no rain cause droughts. Plants, animals, and people often can't get enough water.

When the land is this dry, wildfires are a problem. Wildfires can be triggered by a bolt of lightning or a careless person building a fire. In recent years, wildfires fed by the dry land have become bigger and more frequent than ever before.

Worst Wildfire Season
Australia had its worst wildfire season ever in 2020. Billions of animals lost their homes.

Why Is Climate Change Happening?

Of all the planets in our solar system, Earth is the only one we know of that has life. Part of the reason for that is Earth's atmosphere.

As the Sun's energy passes through Earth's atmosphere, some of that energy is absorbed by Earth's surface. Some of that energy gets released as heat that rises back into the atmosphere.

The atmosphere is made of a mixture of gases. These gases act like a blanket. They trap the rising heat next to Earth's surface. This keeps the planet warm enough to support different kinds of life. But if there is too much of certain gases, problems arise.

One of the gases that traps heat is called carbon dioxide. For a long time, the amount of carbon dioxide in Earth's atmosphere remained pretty steady. But over the past century, it began to rise very rapidly.

Why the increase? It all started about 300 years ago. That was the beginning of the Industrial Revolution, which ushered in a flood of new inventions. Over time, these inventions led to coal-powered factories, steam engines, and gasoline-powered automobiles. All of these things burned fossil fuels, such as coal, oil, and natural gas, for energy. Burning fossil fuels releases carbon dioxide into the atmosphere.

The word "smog" comes from putting together parts of the words "smoke" and "fog."

Today, there are more cars and more factories. There's also much more carbon dioxide in the atmosphere than there was 100 years ago. When sunlight reacts with that carbon dioxide, other gases, and fine particles in the atmosphere, it forms smog. Smog turns the sky gray. It can make people sick, and it can kill plants.

Fossil Fuels

Fossil fuels come from ancient living things. When these organisms died, they were buried under layers of dirt and mud. Over millions of years, heat and pressure changed their remains into fossils.

Strangely, the part of Earth seeing the biggest impact from all of this is a place that has few cars—the Arctic. Temperatures there are rising about three times faster than the rest of the planet.

The Arctic's ice and snow reflect the Sun's energy. This helps to keep Earth's temperatures from getting too high. But as Arctic ice melts, more land is uncovered to release heat. Temperatures rise.

Land not covered by ice in the Arctic is covered by permafrost. This is a thick layer of soil under the surface that remains frozen. Higher temperatures warm the ground so the permafrost thaws. A gas called methane escapes the soft ground and rises into the atmosphere. Like carbon dioxide, methane traps heat. That causes Earth's temperature to creep up even more.

What Are People Doing About Climate Change?

Fortunately, scientists have lots of ideas about how to tackle the problem of climate change. At the top of their list is trying to decrease the amount of carbon dioxide entering Earth's atmosphere. One way to do this is to use new sources of energy that do not rely on fossil fuels. Another is to create new inventions that limit the amount of carbon dioxide released in the atmosphere.

Solar Panels
Solar panels absorb energy from the Sun and change it into electric energy. Wires carry the electricity away from solar panels to homes and businesses.

The spinning blades of a wind turbine turn energy from the wind into electricity.

A big step is using more renewable energy sources to make electricity. Tapping into energy from the Sun, wind, and water releases less carbon dioxide than burning fossil fuels.

The possibilities are amazing. Many new cars, for example, run on electricity. Other cars, buses, and airplanes are powered by fuels made from algae, sugar, and even cooking oil!

Limiting new carbon dioxide emissions is one thing. But how do you take out a gas that's already in the atmosphere? Fortunately, nature has already given us a tool to help conquer that problem—plants!

Plants take carbon dioxide out of the atmosphere and use it to make energy. Replanting forests that have been cut down is one way to soak up some of the carbon dioxide. Planting gardens is another. Garden plants need carbon dioxide to grow, too. And, when more people grow their own vegetables, fewer trucks are needed to carry food from farms to stores. That's a win-win!

What Can You Do About Climate Change?

Despite everything that's being done to fight climate change, there's one more huge challenge. How do you make people understand that climate change is a massive and urgent problem?

The atmosphere surrounds the entire planet. It doesn't matter where extra carbon dioxide comes from. It all ends up in the same place. And it all adds up to one huge problem for Earth.

Greta Thunberg is a climate activist from Sweden. In 2018, she started an international movement to fight climate change.

One thing you can do is to make other people aware of the problem. Help them understand how they can make a difference. Knowledge and awareness are powerful tools in stopping climate change.

Have you ever heard the expression "going green"? Many people say that's what we need to do to save Earth's climate. All it means is changing your own everyday habits to cut down on the amount of carbon dioxide entering Earth's atmosphere.

The easiest thing you can do is to use less energy. Turn off lights when you leave a room. Turn off the TV when you are done watching it. Both of these actions can help your household use less electricity—and save money, too.

What About Water?

Moving water to homes and making it safe to drink takes energy. Turn off the water when you brush your teeth, and take a shorter shower to save energy.

Making new things like clothes and electronics takes energy. You can make a difference by buying used things. Or, you can fix things that are broken rather than throwing them away. Your choices count.

Scientists use the term "carbon footprint" to describe how much carbon dioxide each person generates when they use energy. Choices to use less energy make your carbon footprint smaller.

What choices will you make? Someday, you may choose a career in which you help to solve the problem of climate change. You might be a scientist who discovers a fuel that doesn't release carbon dioxide. Or, you might make an invention that easily absorbs extra carbon dioxide right out of the atmosphere.

In the meantime, learn all you can about the problem. Inspire others to help. And you, too, can do your part to save the climate!

Biggest Carbon Footprints
Highly populated countries like China and the U.S. have the largest total carbon footprints. Some small countries like Qatar and New Caledonia have the largest carbon footprints per person.

Glossary

Absorbed
Soaked up

Atmosphere
A thick layer of gases that
surrounds Earth

Carbon dioxide
A colorless gas made of carbon
and oxygen that helps trap heat
next to Earth

Carbon footprint
The amount of carbon dioxide
produced by a person by
using energy

Climate
The average weather conditions in
an area over a period of years

Drought
A long period with little or
no rainfall

Evidence
The information, observation, or
facts that support a claim

Fossil fuels
Fuels such as coal, oil, or natural
gas made from the remains (fossils)
of ancient plants and animals

Glaciers
Slow-moving rivers of ice formed
at Earth's poles and on
mountaintops

Global warming
The slow increase of Earth's
temperature due to extra carbon
dioxide in the atmosphere

Permafrost
A layer of soil found near Earth's
poles that is always frozen

Reflect
To bounce off

Renewable resource
A resource that can't get used up

Smog
Air pollution made of gases and
fine particles

Weather
The conditions in the atmosphere
at a specific point in time

Index

Quiz

Answer the questions to see what you have learned. Check your answers in the key below.

1. True or False: Weather and climate are the same thing.

2. Are some changes in climate normal?

3. Are the climate changes we are seeing now normal?

4. What does climate change cause that leads to more wildfires?

5. How does too much carbon dioxide in the atmosphere cause climate change?

6. True or False: Energy from the Sun, wind, and water releases as much carbon dioxide as burning coal or oil.

7. What can people do to get rid of excess carbon dioxide in the atmosphere?

8. What do you do when you "go green"?

1. False 2. Yes 3. No 4. Drought 5. Carbon dioxide traps heat next to Earth, and this makes the temperature of Earth's surface get warmer 6. False 7. Plant trees and other kinds of plants 8. Change your everyday habits